CONFIGURING AN ORGANIZATION WITHIN DYNAMICS AX 2012

BY MURRAY FIFE

ISBN: 1499748817

ISBN-13: 978-1499748819

Preface

What you need for this Blueprint

All the examples shown in this blueprint were done with the Microsoft Dynamics AX 2012 virtual machine image that was downloaded from the Microsoft CustomerSource or PartnerSource site. If you don't have your own installation of Microsoft Dynamics AX 2012, you can also use the images found on the Microsoft Learning Download Center. The following list of software from the virtual image was leveraged within this blueprint:

*   Microsoft Dynamics AX 2012

Even though all the preceding software was used during the development and testing of the recipes in this book, they may also work on earlier versions of the software with minor tweaks and adjustments, and should also work on later versions without any changes.

Errata

Although we have taken every care to ensure the accuracy of our content, mistakes do happen. If you find a mistake in one of our books—maybe a mistake in the text or the code—we would be grateful if you would report this to us. By doing so, you can save other readers from frustration and help us improve subsequent versions of this book. If you find any errata, please report them by emailing murray@murrayfife.me.

Piracy

Piracy of copyright material on the Internet is an ongoing problem across all media. If you come across any illegal copies of our works, in any form, on the Internet, please provide us with the location address or website name immediately so that we can pursue a remedy.

Please contact us at murray@murrayfife.me with a link to the suspected pirated material.

We appreciate your help in protecting our authors, and our ability to bring you valuable content.

Questions

You can contact us at murray@murrayfife.me if you are having a problem with any aspect of the book, and we will do our best to address it.

Table Of Contents

INTRODUCTION

Before we start configuring all of the main areas of Dynamics AX like Human Resources, Sales, General Ledger etc. we need to pause for a little bit and configure the parent **Organization** details. A lot of the information that we will be configuring here is used throughout the system, and it's a good idea to get this out of the way before we move on to the real application.

The following guide will step you through the bare necessities that you will need to configure within the **Organization Administration** area of Dynamics AX so the rest of your journey through the application is smooth sailing.

CONFIGURING YOUR ORGANIZATION

There are a few additional configuration steps to the Organizations codes and controls that you will want to do before continuing on to the rest of the system. These will be global configurations that help all of the other modules work smoothly.

In this chapter we will step through what you need to do to.

Initialize the Organizations Number Sequences

The **Number Sequences** within Dynamics AX are used to index all of the records and transactions, and almost any record within Dynamics AX has a related **Number Sequence**. Unfortunately when you first create a blank organization, there are almost no number sequences that are created by default. So the first task that you should do is create them. Fortunately that's not a big deal, because you can just run a quick wizard, and it will create the 100+ number sequences for you.

Initialize the Organizations Number Sequences

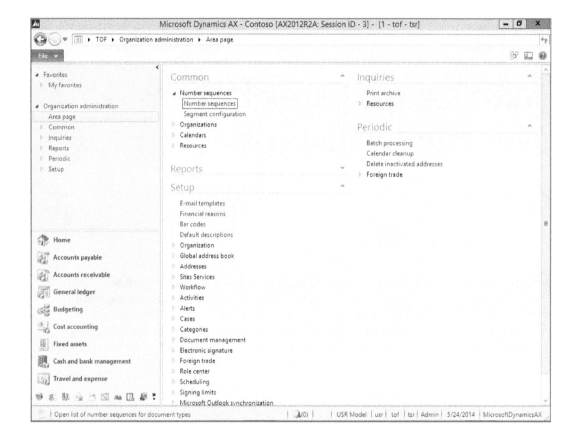

To do this, click on the **Number Sequences** menu item within the **Number Sequences** folder of the **Common** group within the **Organizational Administration** area page.

Initialize the Organizations Number Sequences

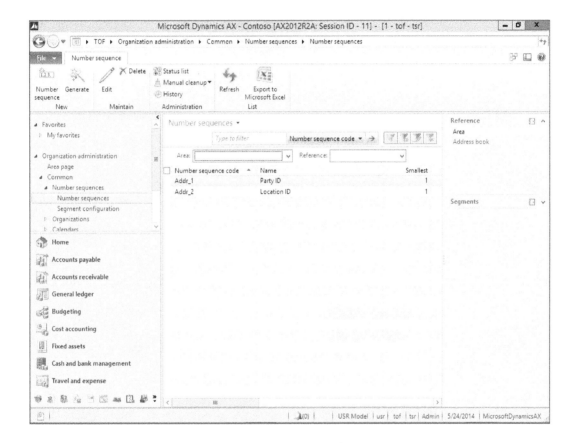

When the **Number Sequences** list page is displayed, click on the **Generate** button within the **New** group of the **Number Sequences** action panel.

Initialize the Organizations Number Sequences

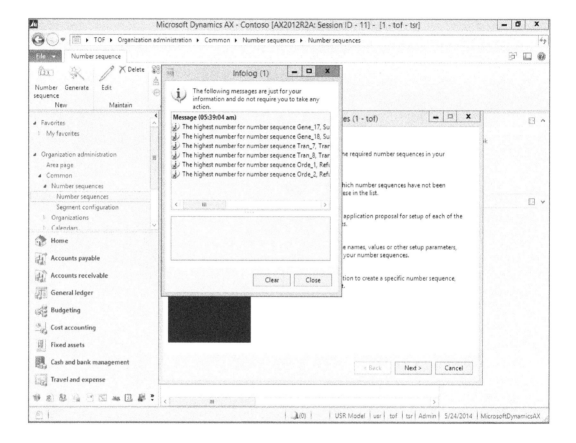

Dynamics AX will then show a few messages to do with numbering ranges, just click the **Close** button to continue on.

Initialize the Organizations Number Sequences

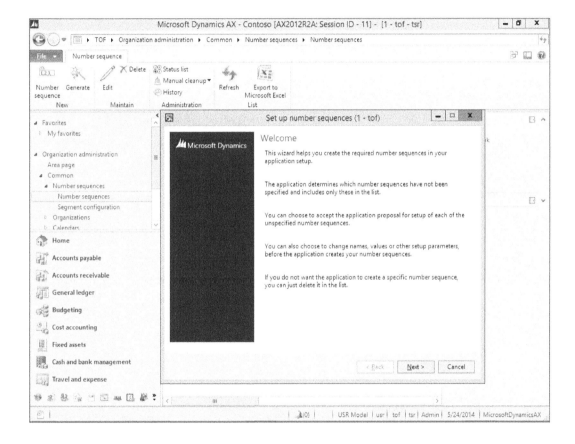

When the Set Up **Number Sequence** wizard is displayed, click **Next** to step to the next page.

Initialize the Organizations Number Sequences

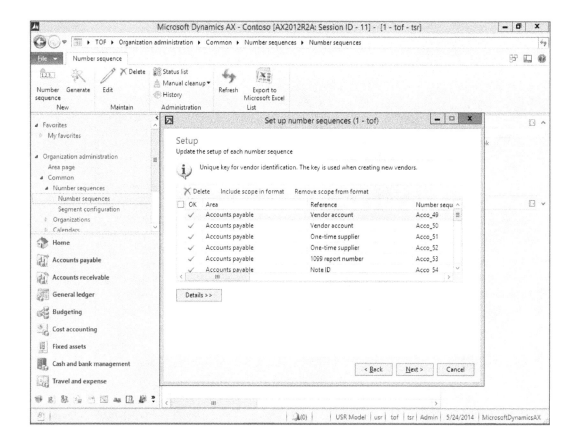

The next page will show you all of the default number sequences that Dynamics AX will create for you. If you just have a single organization then you can click the **Next** button to continue on.

Initialize the Organizations Number Sequences

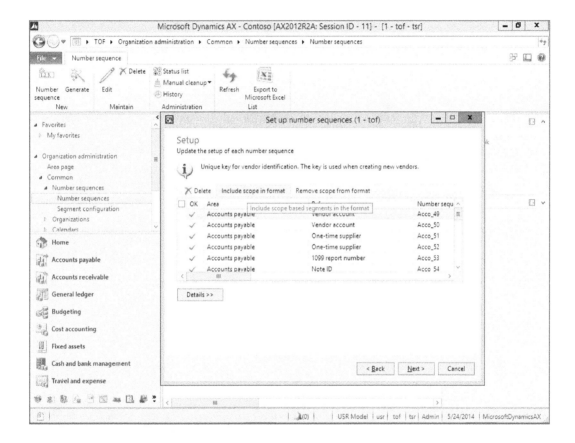

If you are going to have multiple legal entities, then you may want to click on the **Include Scope In Format** button in the action panel.

Initialize the Organizations Number Sequences

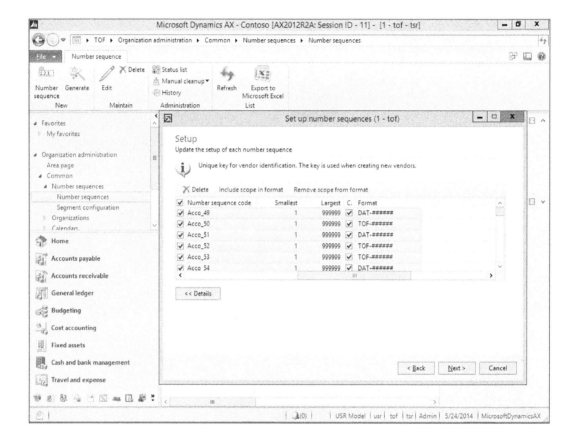

If you click on the **Details** button it will then show you that the organization id is included in the number formats, providing a little more segregation between the organizations, and removes the chance of number sequence duplication between organizations.

Initialize the Organizations Number Sequences

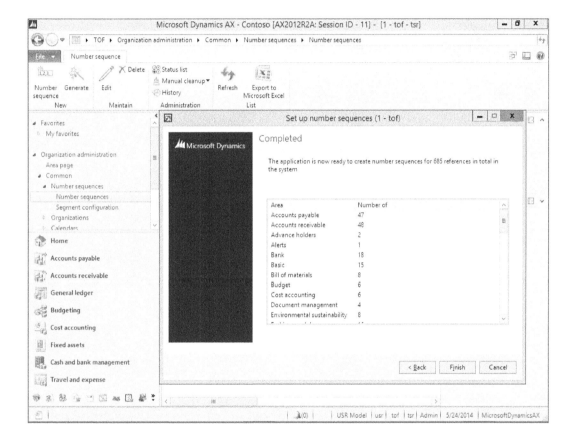

When the final page is displayed, you will see a summary of all the number sequences that are going to be created, and to create them, just click on the **Finish** button.

Initialize the Organizations Number Sequences

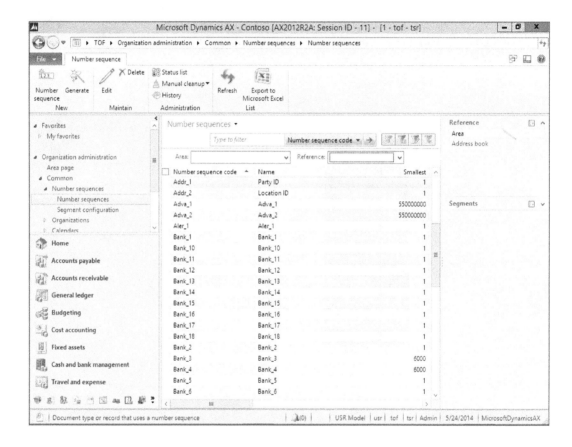

Now when you return to the **Number Sequences** list page you will see that you have a lot more records.

Importing Address Zip Code, City, State & County Components

When the initial organization data is created, Dynamics AX does not populate any of the standard postal code, city, state or county information – probably because it would be immediately out of date. So another housekeeping task that you will probably want to perform is to import in the address components which will then allow you to validate your addresses as you start entering them in.

Importing Address Zip Code, City, State & County Components

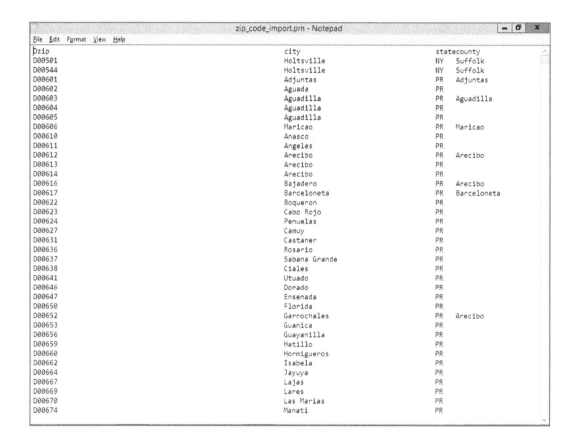

The first thing that you will need to do is create an import file for your address components. You need to get an list of all the zip codes, and then format the data in a fixed length delimited file. You can do this yourself, or you can save time, and grab the file from my resources page.

http://www.murrayfife.me/resources

Importing Address Zip Code, City, State & County Components

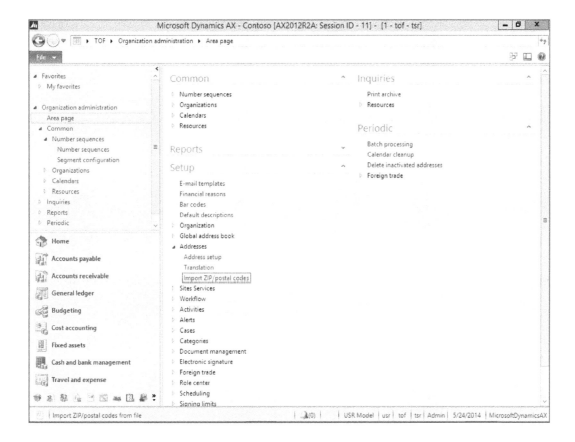

Then click on the **Import Zip/Portal Codes** menu item within the **Addresses** folder of the **Setup** group within the **Organization Administration** area page.

Importing Address Zip Code, City, State & County Components

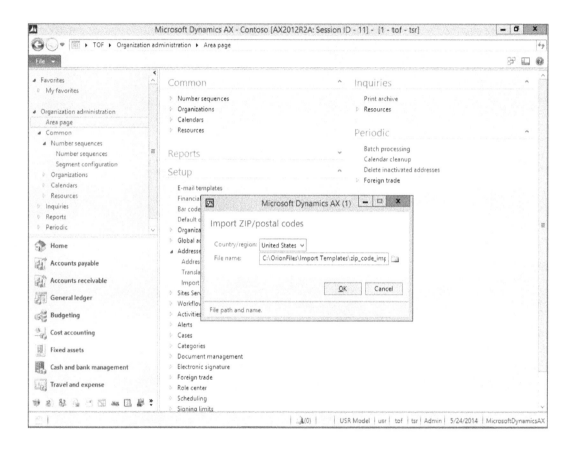

When the **Import Zip/Postal Code** dialog box is displayed, select the **Country/Region** that you are importing the address components for, and then point the **File Name** to where you have stored your zip code import file. When you have done that, just click on the **OK** button.

Importing Address Zip Code, City, State & County Components

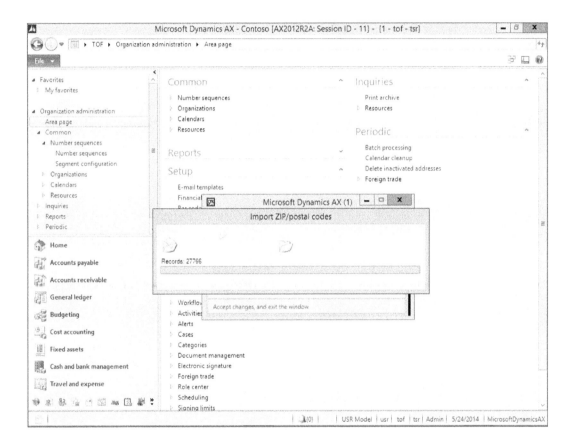

Dynamics AX will then start processing the zip codes and adding them to the database.

Importing Address Zip Code, City, State & County Components

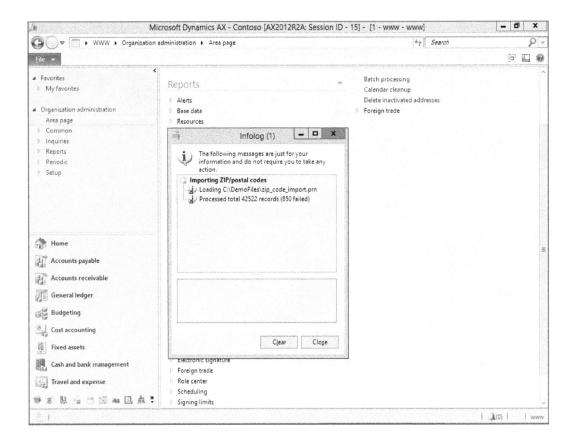

If there are any inconsistencies within the import file, then you will get a notice.

Importing Address Zip Code, City, State & County Components

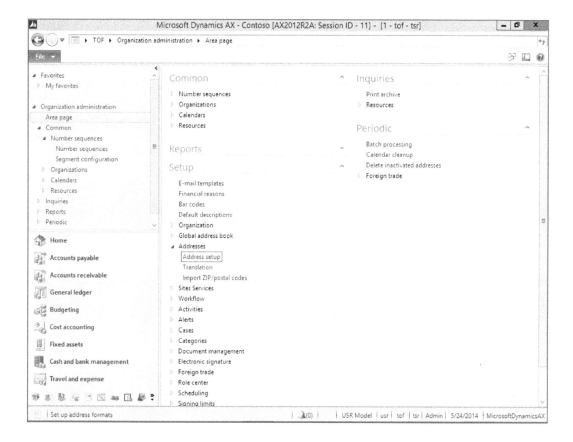

Now you can view all of the address components. To do this click on the **Address Setup** menu item within the **Addresses** folder of the **Setup** group within the **Organization Administration** area page.

Importing Address Zip Code, City, State & County Components

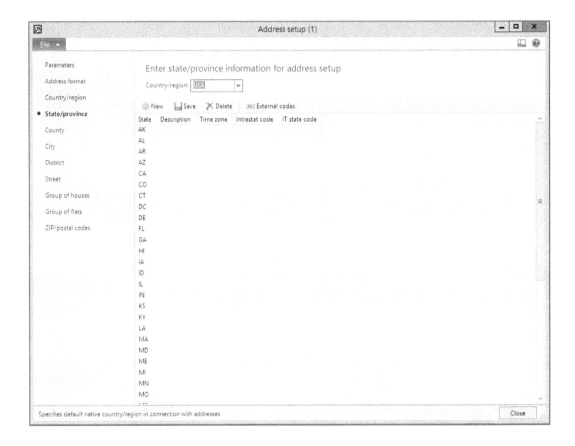

When the **Address** Setup form is displayed, click on the **State/Province** page, and then select **Country/Region** code that you imported in the data for. This will show you all of your states. Unfortunately you need to still fill in all of the state descriptions, but that's not a lot of work.

Importing Address Zip Code, City, State & County Components

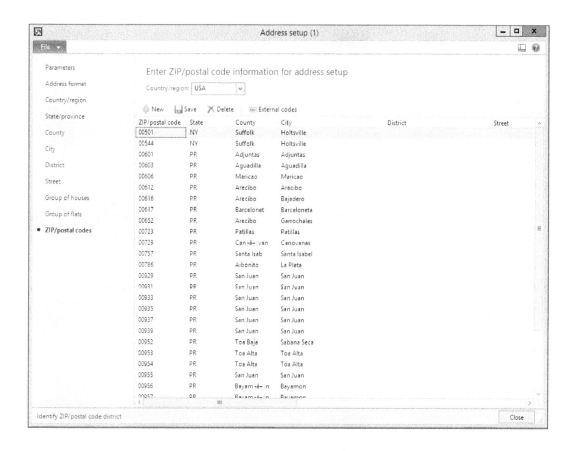

If you click on the **ZIP/Postal Codes** page you will see that all of the zip codes should now be populated along with the **State**, **City**, and **County** relationships.

Importing Address Zip Code, City, State & County Components

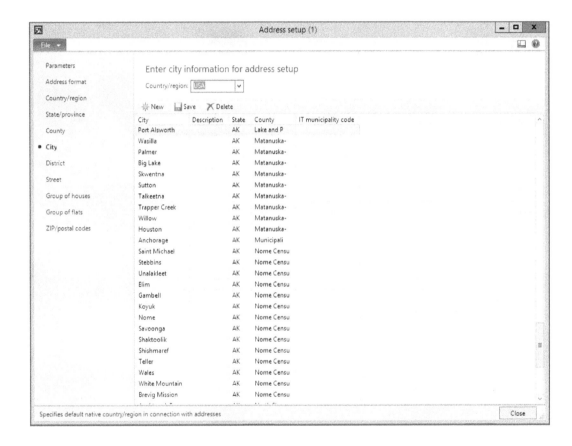

Also all of the **City** data is loaded as well.

When you are happy that the address details have been loaded, click on the **Close** button to exit from the form.

Configuring The Global Address Book Properties

The **Global Address Book** contains all of the contact information for all of the people and places that you will be referencing within Dynamics AX. Before you start creating contacts though you can save yourself a lot of time in data tweaking by setting a couple of default within the **Global Address Book Parameters**.

Configuring The Global Address Book Properties

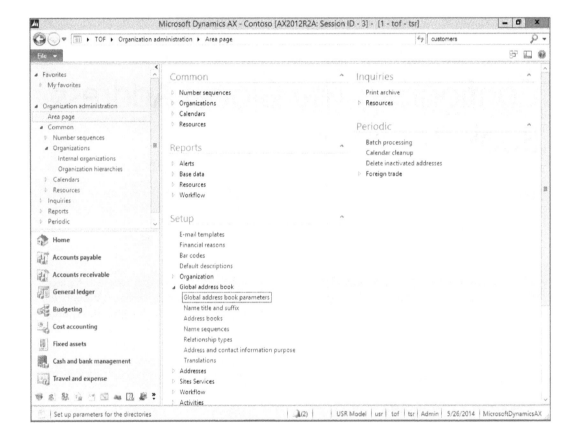

To do this, click on the **Global Address Book Parameters** menu item within the **Global Address Book** folder of the **Setup** group within the **Organization Administration** area page.

Configuring The Global Address Book Properties

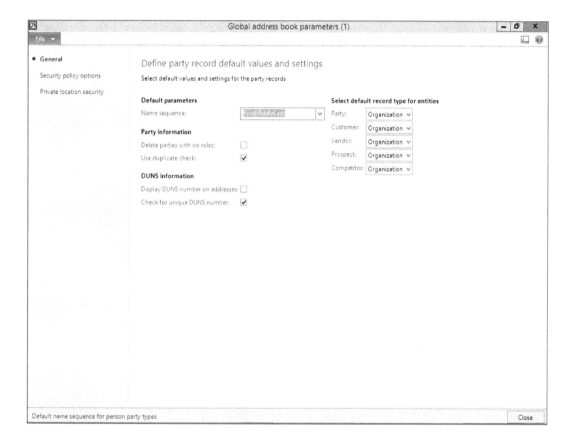

When the **Global Address Book Parameters** maintenance page is displayed, select the **General** page.

Configuring The Global Address Book Properties

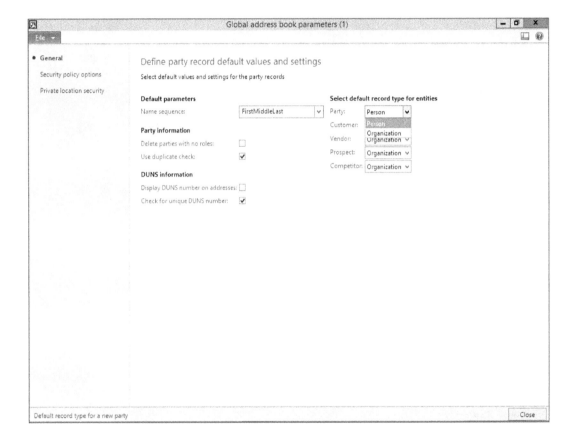

When a Global Address Book record (either a **Person** or an **Organization**) is created within the system, by default it will suggest that you are creating an **Organization**. This is fine if you are a B2B organization, but if you are interacting with people for the most part, then you may want to change the default record types to **Person**. To do this, just select the record type from the dropdown box within the **Select Default Record Type For Entities** group.

Configuring The Global Address Book Properties

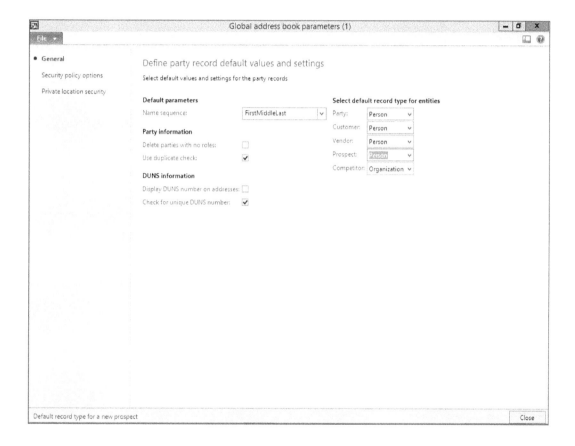

Note: You can mix and match the Organization and Person defaults for all of the different entities.

Configuring The Global Address Book Properties

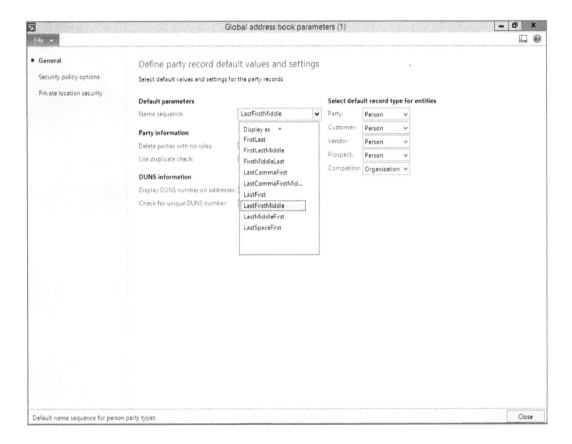

Also, when you create a new **Person** record type in the global address book, Dynamics AX will create a default description for them. You may want to have this displayed the default way which is **First Name**, **Middle Name**, and then **Last Name**, but if you're like me then you may want to change this to **Last Name**, **First Name**, and then **Middle Name** by changing the **Name Sequence** field.

Configuring The Global Address Book Properties

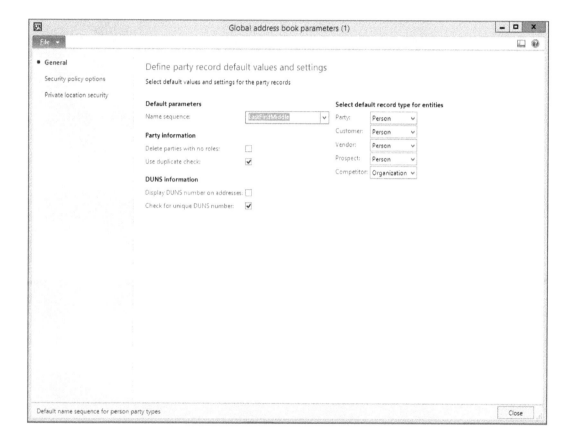

Once you have done that, click on the **Close** button to exit from the form.

Configuring Default Address Books

Address Books within Dynamics AX are a great way for you to segregate out all of your contacts into different groups, and also to secure your contacts so that only certain people have access to the contacts. So a good idea is to configure a few default **Address Books** so that later on as you start creating contacts, you can assign them to different groups.

Configuring Default Address Books

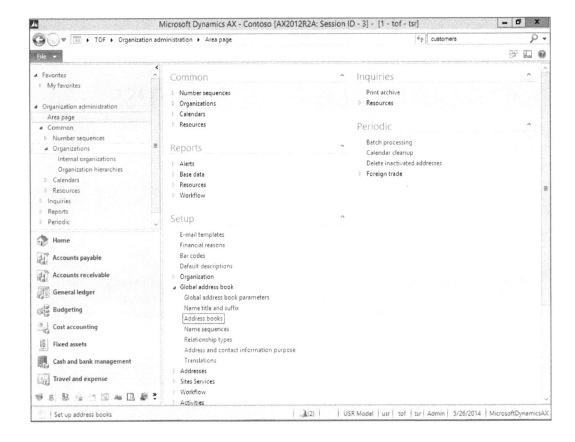

To do this, click on the **Address Books** menu item within the **Global Address Book** folder of the **Setup** group within the **Organization Administration** area page.

Configuring Default Address Books

When the **Address Books** maintenance page is displayed, click on the **New** button in the menu bar to create a new record.

Configuring Default Address Books

Then assign your **Address Book** a **Name** and a **Description.**

Configuring Default Address Books

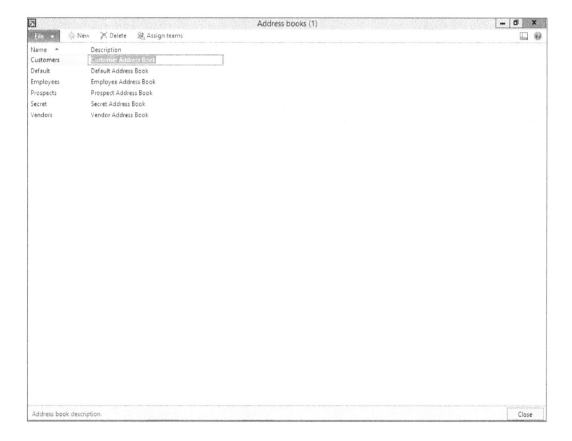

Continue adding additional **Address Books** if you like and when you are done, click on the **Close** button to exit from the form.

Configure Working Time Templates

Another area that you will probably want to configure within the organization is the default working calendars which you will reference a lot when it comes to scheduling, shipping etc. Before we set that up though we need to define a **Working Time Template** that we will use to specify how many hours we will work a day, and also what days we will work.

Configure Working Time Templates

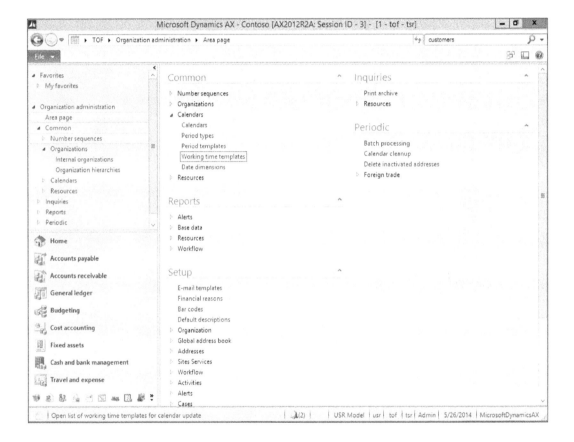

To do this, click on the **Working Time Templates** menu item within the **Calendars** folder of the **Common** group within the **Organization Administration** area page.

Configure Working Time Templates

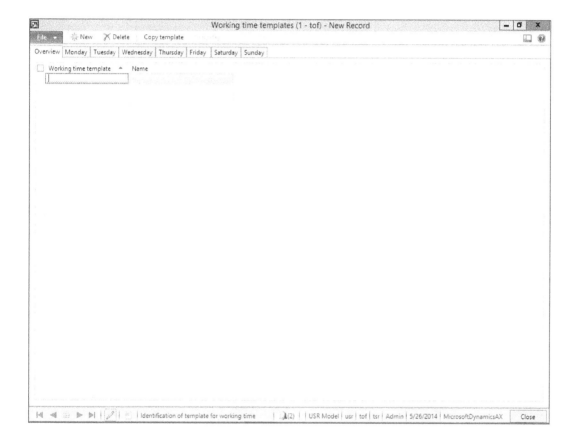

When the **Working Time Templates** maintenance form is displayed, click on **New** button in the menu bar to create a new record.

Configure Working Time Templates

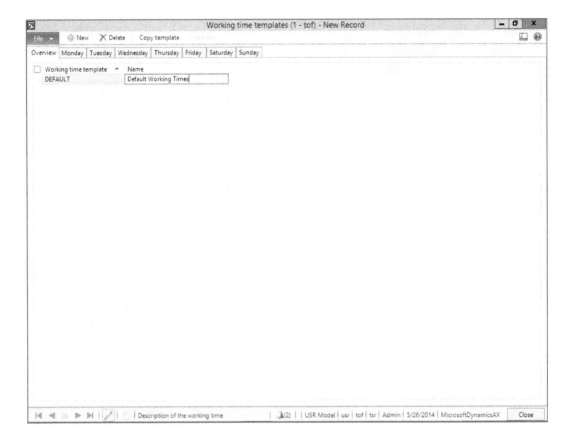

Assign your new record a **Working Time Template** code and a **Name**.

Configure Working Time Templates

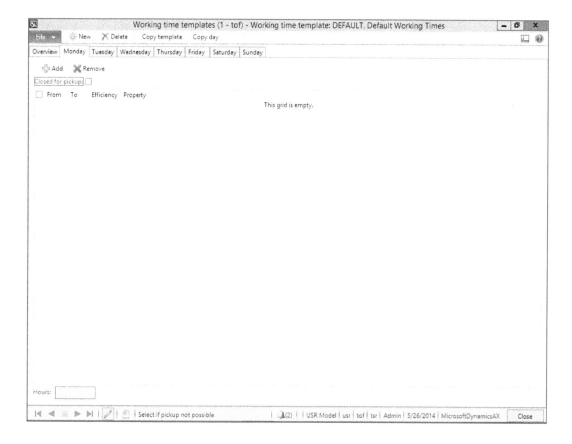

Then switch to the first working day tab that you want to configure working hours for. In this case it's Monday.

Configure Working Time Templates

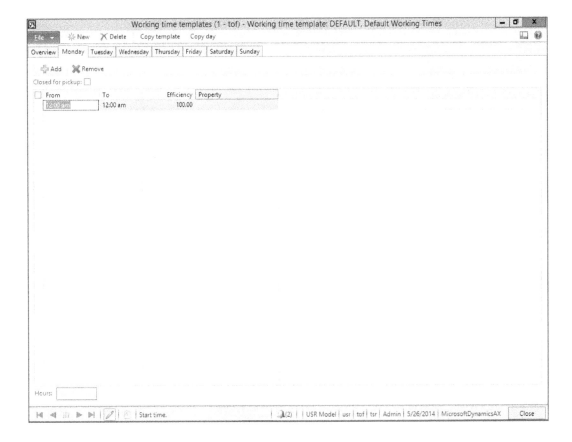

Click on the **Add** button to create a new working time period.

Configure Working Time Templates

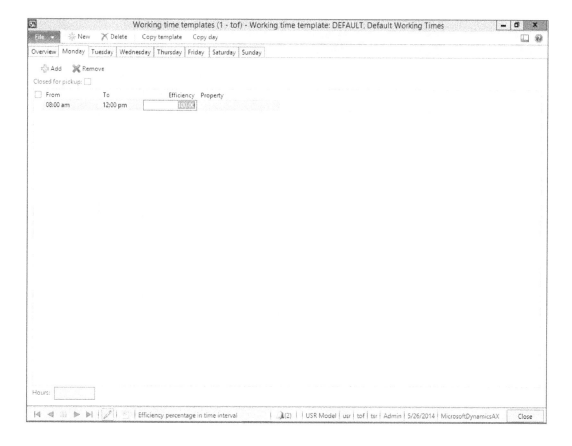

Then type in the **From** time, the **To** time and then also the **Efficiency** percentage.

Configure Working Time Templates

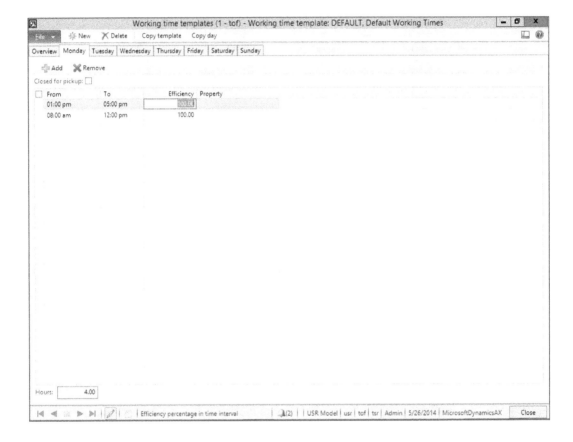

If you have multiple shifts or periods within the day then you can add additional time ranges.

Configure Working Time Templates

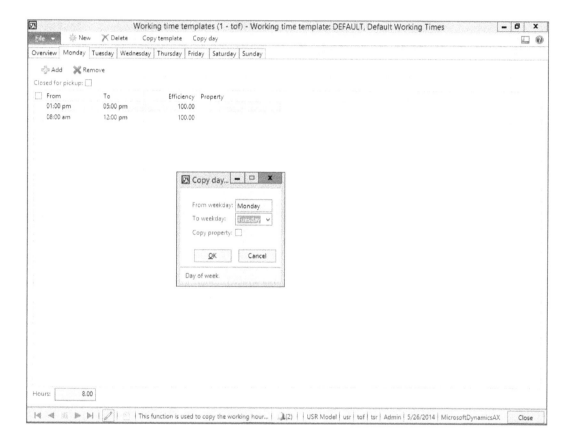

Rather than do this for each day, once you have your first day configured, you can click on the **Copy Day** button in the menu bar which will open up a **Copy Day** dialog box and you can select the next day that you want to copy to.

Configure Working Time Templates

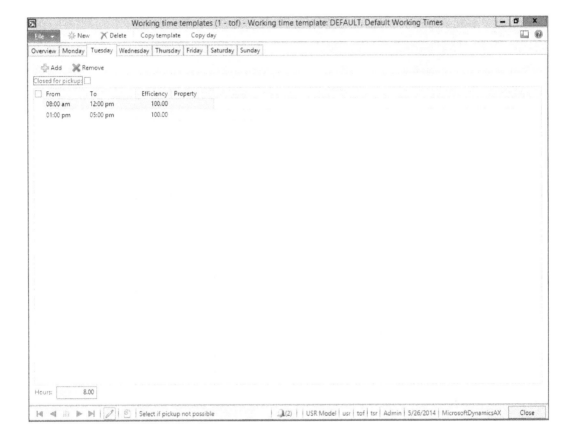

And this will copy the same time periods to the second day.

Configure Working Time Templates

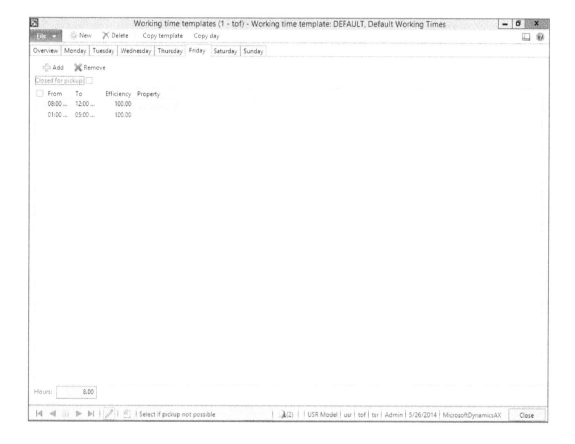

Now you just need to repeat the copy function for all of the other days that you want to work on.

When you are done, then click on the **Close** button to exit from the form.

Configuring Your Organizational Calendar

Once you have configured your working time template you can then use it to create a default **Organizational Calendar** that you can use throughout the application.

Configuring Your Organizational Calendar

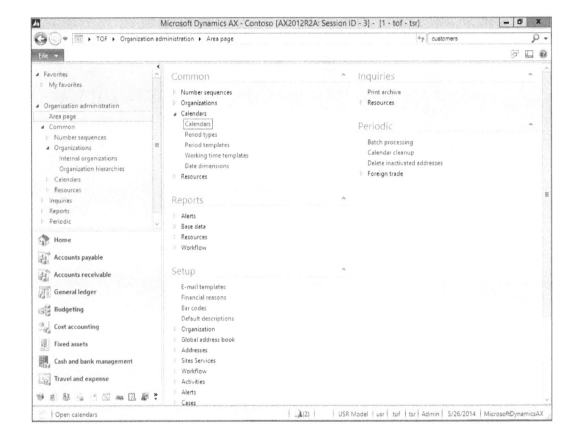

To do this, click on the **Calendars** menu item within the **Calendars** folder of the **Setup** group within the **Organization Administration** area page.

Configuring Your Organizational Calendar

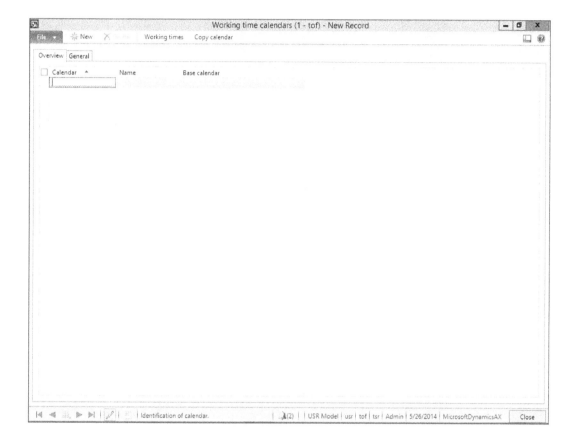

When The **Working Time Calendars** maintenance form is displayed, click on the **New** button in the menu bar to create a new record.

Configuring Your Organizational Calendar

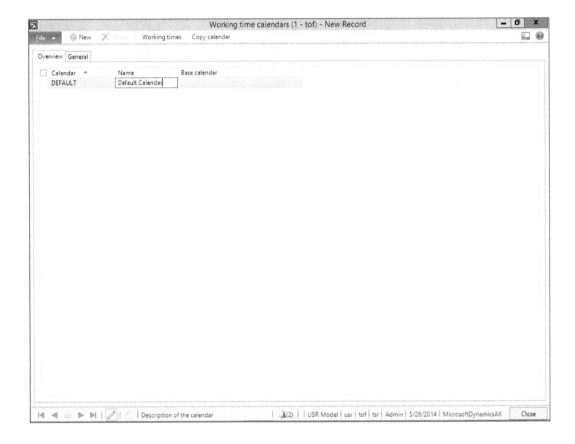

Give your new record a **Calendar** code and also a **Name.**

Configuring Your Organizational Calendar

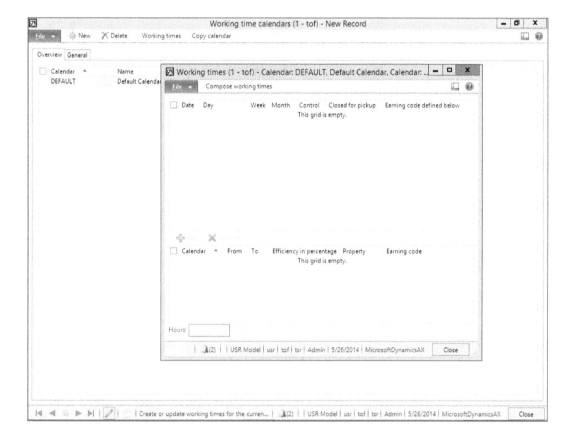

Then click on the **Working Times** button in the menu bar.

Then the **Working Times** maintenance form is displayed, click on the **Compose Working Times** button in the menu bar.

Configuring Your Organizational Calendar

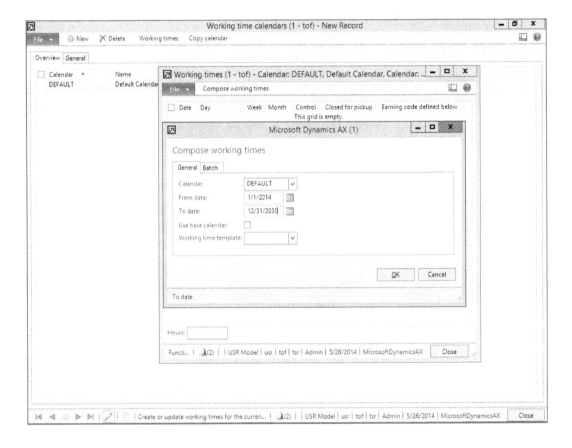

When the **Compose Working Times** dialog box is displayed, select the **From Date** and **To Date** that you want to set up your calendar for.

Configuring Your Organizational Calendar

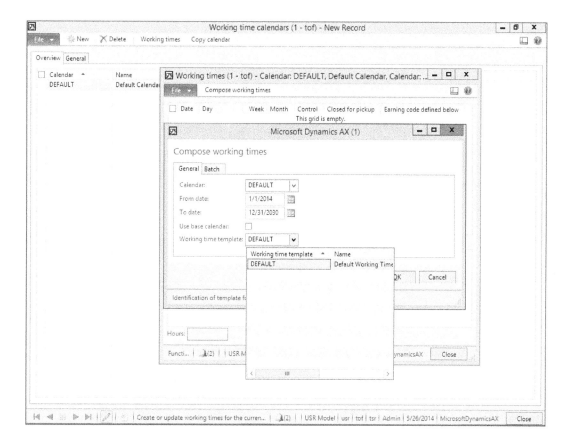

Then from the **Working Time Template** dropdown, select the template that you just configured in the previous step.

Configuring Your Organizational Calendar

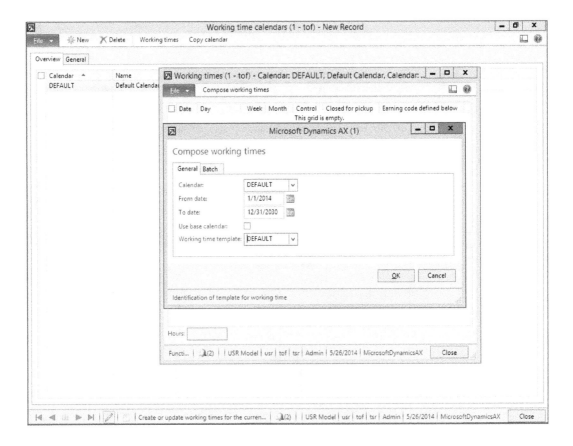

When you have done that, click on the **OK** button to create your calendar.

Configuring Your Organizational Calendar

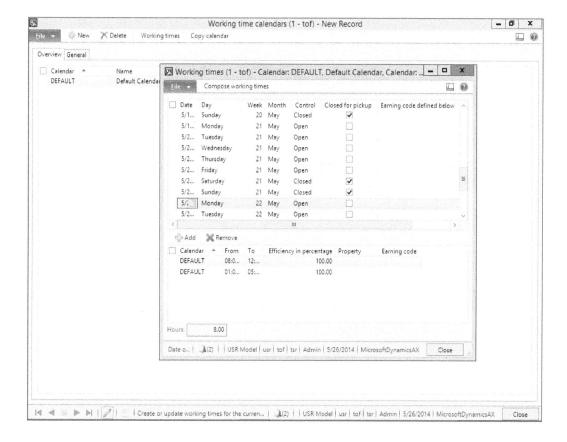

When you return to the **Working Times** maintenance form you will see all of your working days have been populated along with the working times.

You can manually adjust any of the days and times, but for now you can just click the **Close** button to exit from the form.

Creating A Default Email Template

If you are going to send alerts through e-mail, or If you are going to have workflows notify people via e-mail as well, then you will want to first configure a default **Email Template** for Dynamics AX to use.

Creating A Default Email Template

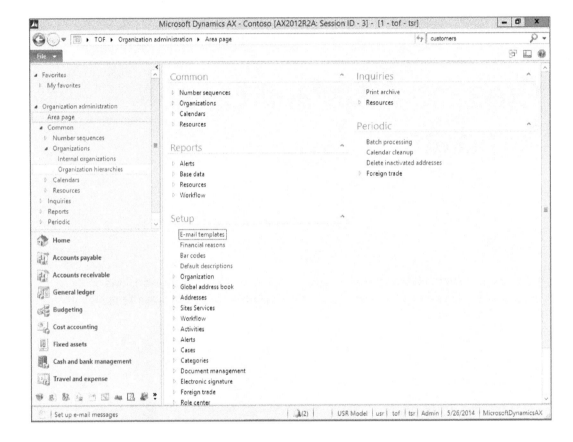

To do this, click on the **E-Mail Templates** menu item within the **Setup** group of the **Organization Administration** area page.

Creating A Default Email Template

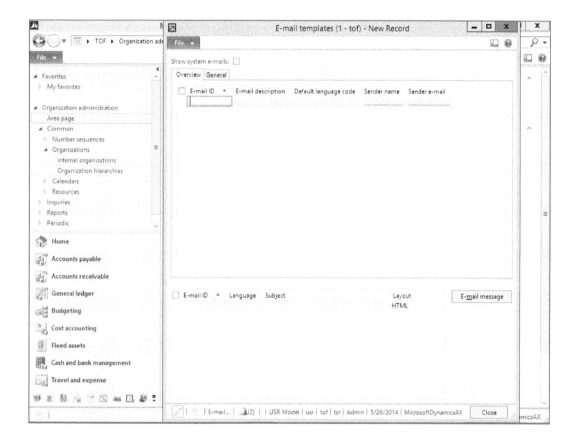

When the **E-Mail Templates** maintenance form is displayed, create a new record by pressing **CTRL+N**.

Creating A Default Email Template

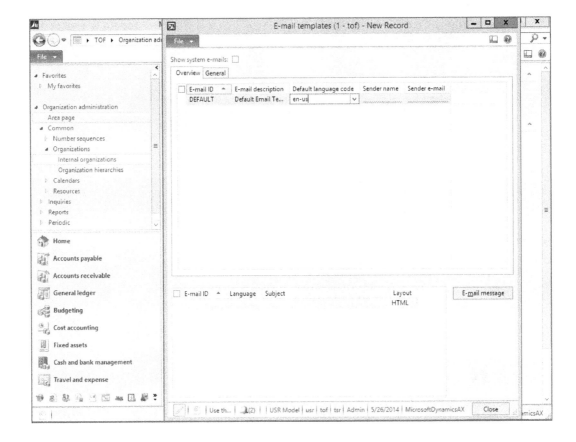

Assign your template a **E-Mail ID**, a **E-Mail Description** and also a **Default Language Code**.

Creating A Default Email Template

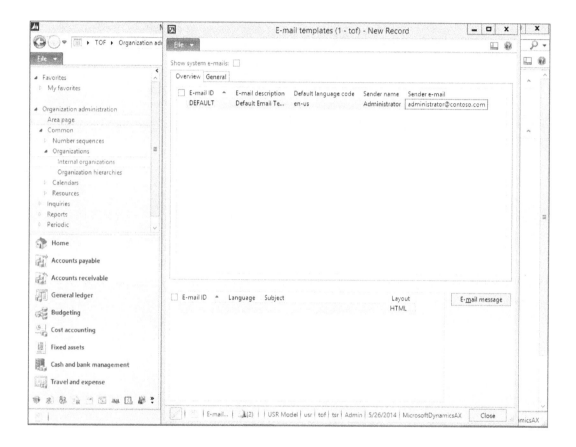

Then also specify a default **Senders Name**, and also a **Senders E-Mail** address.

Creating A Default Email Template

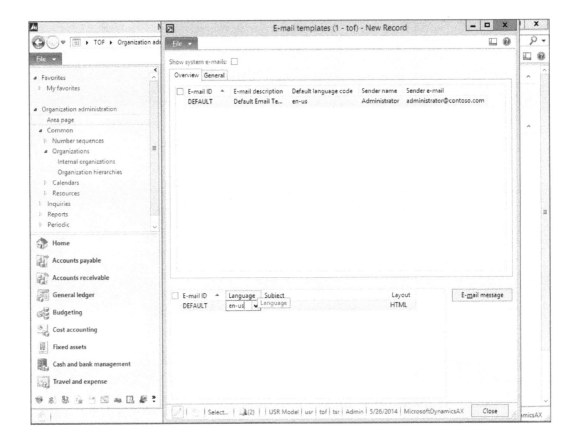

In the lower portion of the form assign your E-Mail template a **Language**.

Note: Even though you have defined the default language code for the email template in the header, you can create multiple versions of the e-mail template itself with different language codes in the lower section.

Creating A Default Email Template

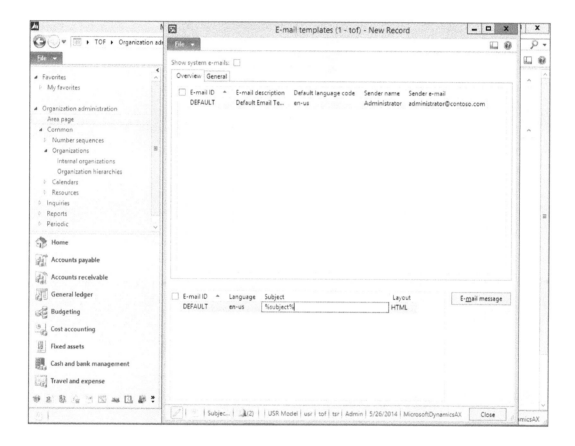

You can type in a generic **Subject** value, or if you want to be clever, type in **%subject%** as a placeholder, and this will tell Dynamics AX to replace it with whatever the subject of the e-mail is that is being sent from the alert of workflow message.

Then click on the **E-Mail Message** button in the lower half of the form to create the e-mail template itself.

Creating A Default Email Template

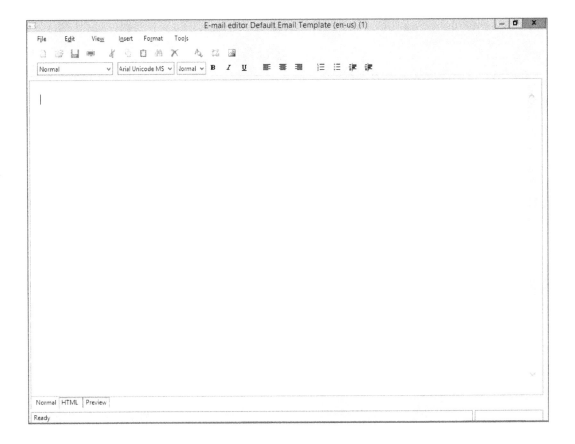

This will open up the **E-Mail Editor** where you can type in your generic e-mail message text.

Creating A Default Email Template

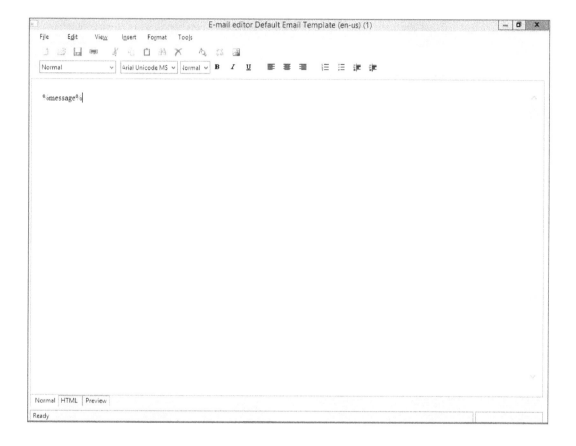

But as with the **Subject** it's a better idea to put a placeholder here if **%message%** so that Dynamics AX will replace it with whatever the body of the e-mail is that is being sent from the alert of workflow message.

When you have done this, close the editor.

Creating A Default Email Template

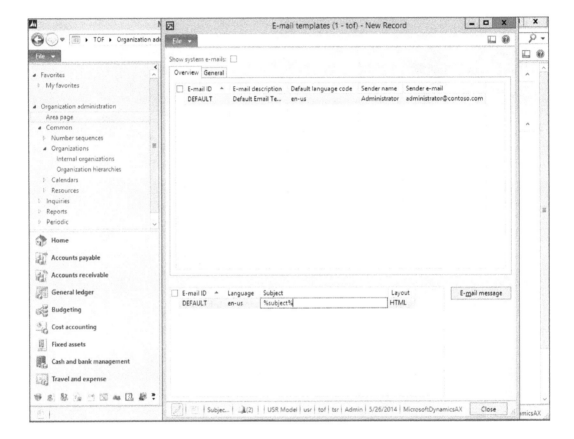

Now you are done, and you can exit from the form by clicking on the **Close** button.

Configuring Your Default Workflow Parameters

You are most definitely going to be using the workflow later on in your setup, so now is a good idea to configure the **Workflow Parameters**.

Configuring Your Default Workflow Parameters

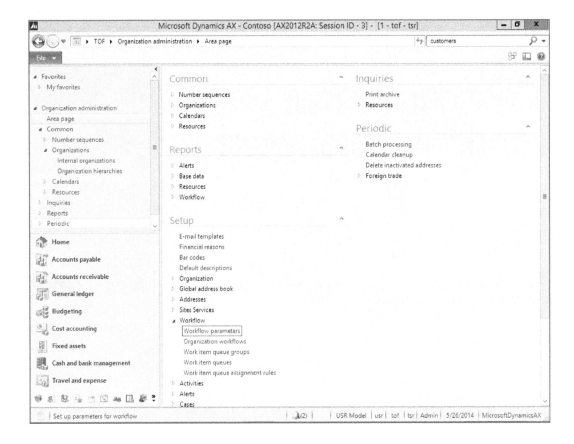

To do this, click on the **Workflow Parameters** menu item within the **Workflow** folder of the **Setup** group within the **Organization Administration** area page.

Configuring Your Default Workflow Parameters

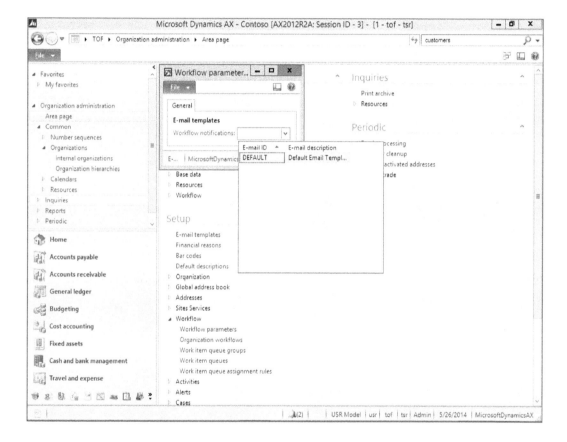

When the **Workflow Parameters** dialog box is displayed, select your default E-Mail Template that you just created from the **Workflow Notification** dropdown list.

Configuring Your Default Workflow Parameters

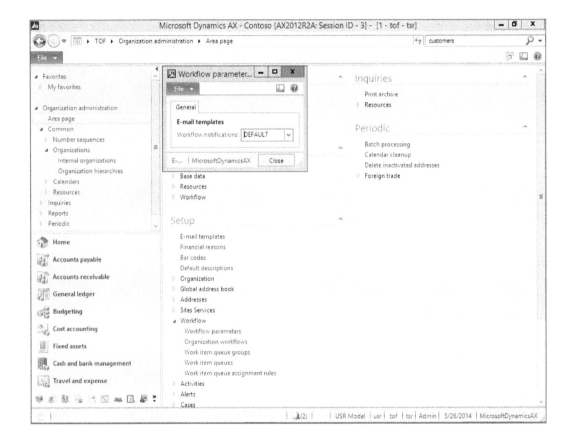

After you have done that, just click on the **Close** button and you are done.

Configure The Alert Notification Parameters

Additionally you will want to now link your E-Mail template to your alert notifications so that if it sends an e-mail then it knows how to format it.

Configure The Alert Notification Parameters

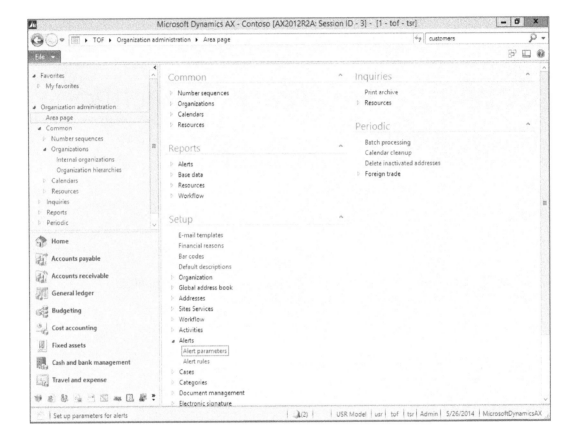

To do this, click on the **Alert Parameters** menu item within the **Alerts** folder of the **Setup** group of the **Organization Administration** area page.

Configure The Alert Notification Parameters

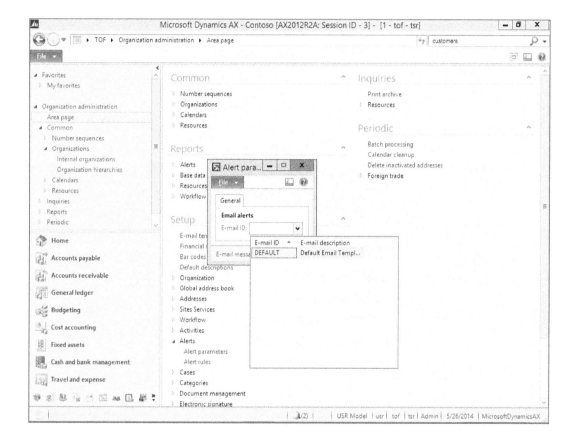

When the **Alert Parameters** dialog box is displayed, select your default E-Mail Template that you just created from the **E-Mail ID** dropdown list.

Configure The Alert Notification Parameters

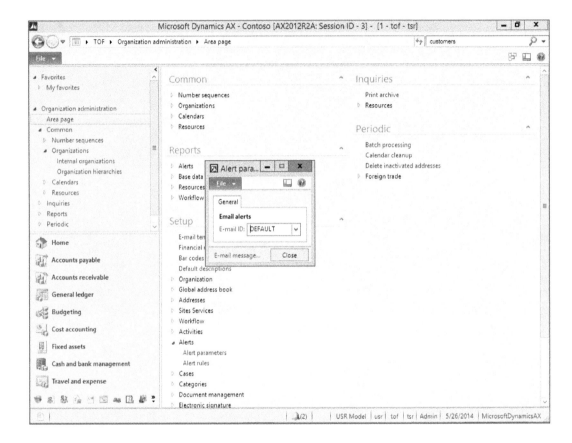

After you have done that, just click on the **Close** button and you are done.

CONFIGURING YOUR LEGAL ENTITY

While you are still within the Organization Administration area, you may also want to make a couple of tweaks to the default Legal Entity that was created to add a little more detail.

In this chapter we will show you some of the initial personalization of the Legal Entity.

Adding an Address to the Legal Entity

Since you have the **address components** configured, you can now add the default corporate address to the Organization details.

Adding an Address to the Legal Entity

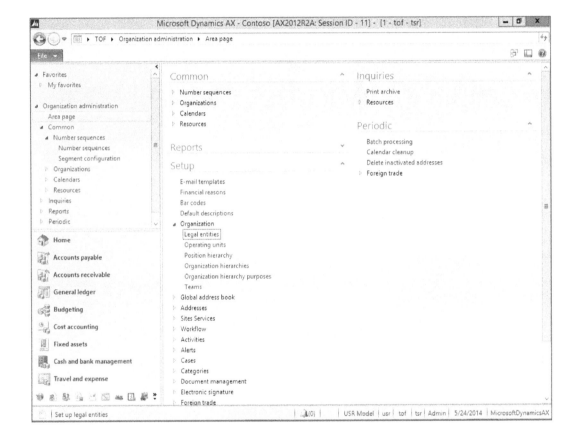

To do this, click on the **Legal Entities** menu item within the **Organization** folder of the **Setup** group within the **Organization Administration** area page.

Adding an Address to the Legal Entity

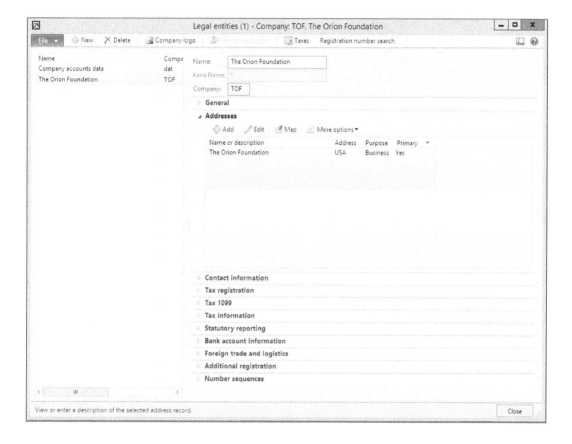

When the **Legal Entities** maintenance form is displayed, select your organization, and then expand the **Addresses** fast tab so that you can see the default address for the organization. There will be a placeholder address there already, and to add the full address, click on the **Edit** button within the menu bar of the **Addresses** fast tab.

Adding an Address to the Legal Entity

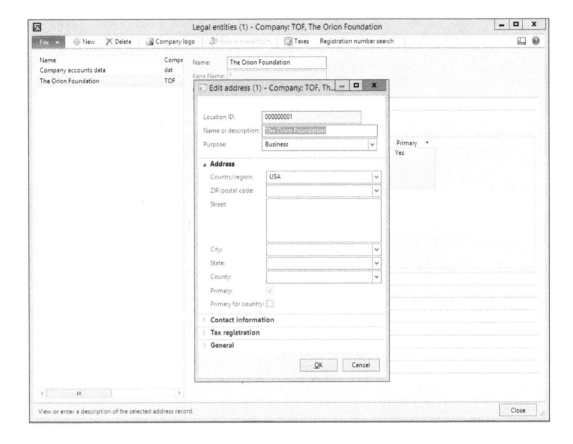

This will open up an address editor.

Adding an Address to the Legal Entity

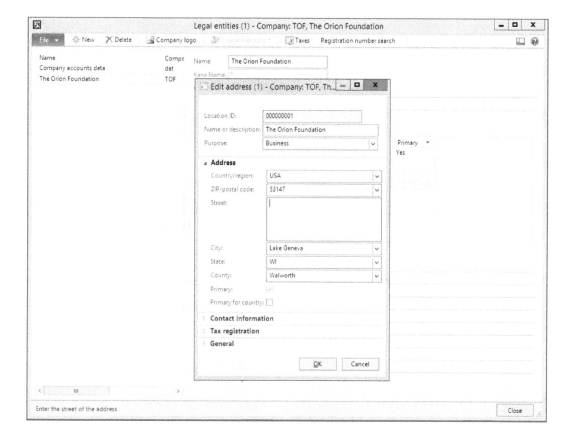

Notice that when you type in a **Zip/Postal Code** Dynamics AX will automatically populate the **City**, **State**, and **County** now that you have the address components loaded.

Adding an Address to the Legal Entity

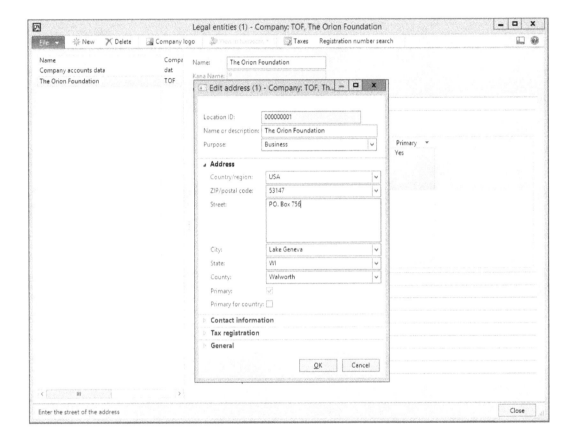

All you need to do is fill in the **Street** and then click on the **OK** button to save the address.

Adding an Address to the Legal Entity

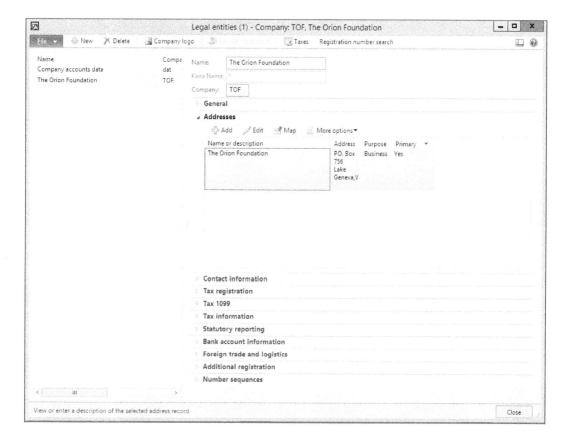

Now when you return to the **Legal Entity** maintenance form you will see that the address details are now showing with the proper address.

You can also keep on adding addresses if you like, and when you are done, just click on the **Close** button to exit from the form.

Adding A Logo To Your Legal Entity

You can attach corporate logos to any of the legal entities within Dynamics AX, and these will automatically be displayed on the forms like the sales order, purchase order etc.

Adding A Logo To Your Legal Entity

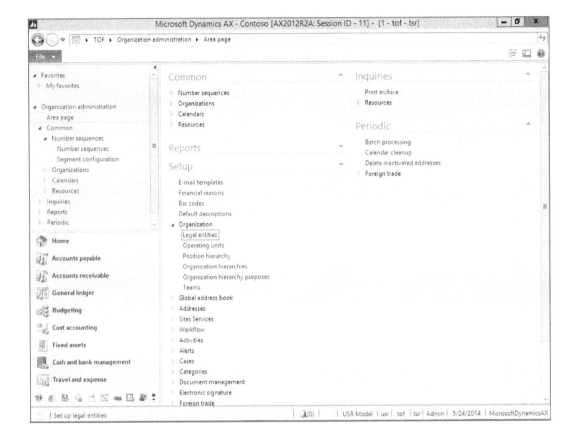

To do this, click on the **Legal Entities** menu item within the **Organization** folder of the **Setup** group within the **Organization Administration** area page.

Adding A Logo To Your Legal Entity

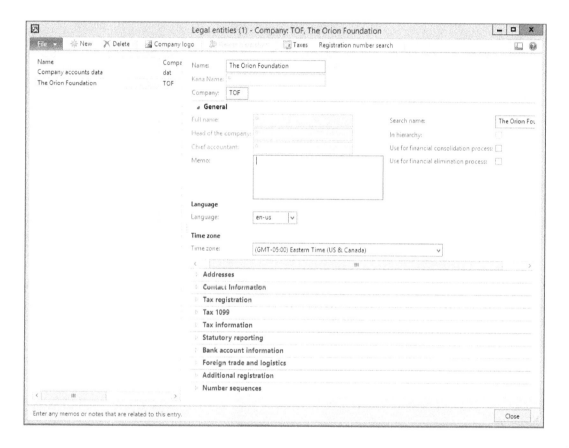

When the **Legal Entities** maintenance form is displayed, select the company that you want to add a logo to and then click on the **Company Logo** menu item within the menu bar.

Adding A Logo To Your Legal Entity

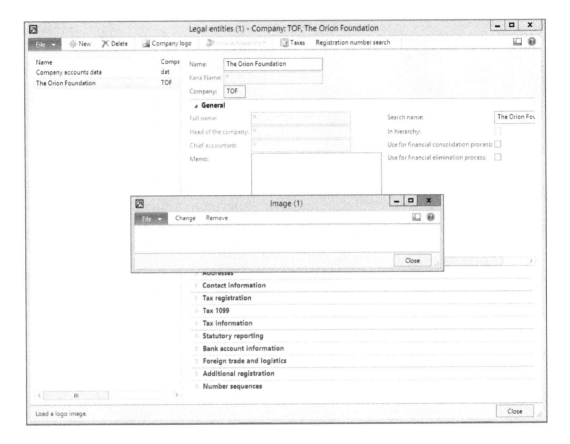

When the **Image** dialog box is displayed, click on the **Change** button within the menu bar.

Adding A Logo To Your Legal Entity

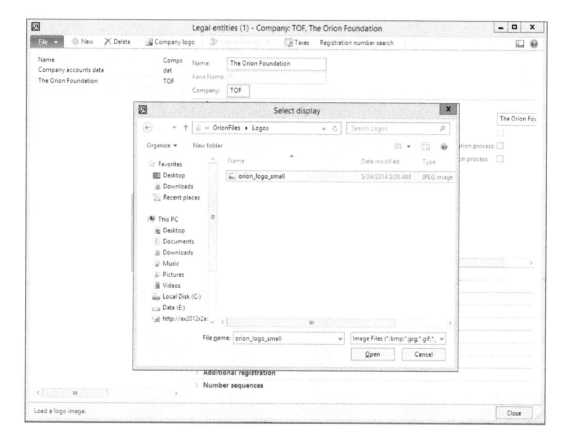

Then navigate to the company logo file that you want to use and click on the **Open** button.

Adding A Logo To Your Legal Entity

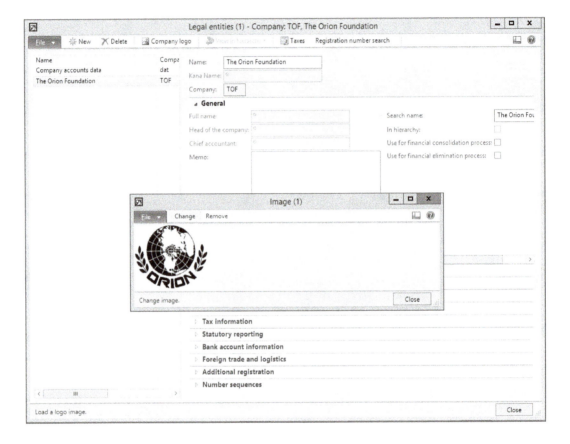

When you return back to the **Image** dialog box, you will see the logo is now associated with the legal entity.

Tip: Don't make this logo too big, because it shows up in life sized form on the documents. Sometimes bigger is not better.

When you are done, click on the **Close** button and exit out of the forms.

SUMMARY

Now that you have your **Organization** configured you can start getting to the meal and potatoes of the application and start setting up some real data.

About the Author

Murray Fife is a Microsoft Dynamics AX MVP, and Author with over 20 years of experience in the software industry.

Like most people in this industry he has paid his dues as a developer, an implementation consultant, a trainer, and now spend most of his days working with companies solving their problems with the Microsoft suite of products, specializing in the Dynamics® AX solutions.

EMAIL	murray@murrayfife.me
TWITTER	@murrayfife
SKYPE	murrayfife
AMAZON	http://www.amazon.com/author/murrayfife
BLOG	http://dynamicsaxtipoftheday.com
	http://extendingdynamicsax.com
	http://atinkerersnotebook.com
SLIDESHARE	http://slideshare.net/murrayfife
LINKEDIN	http://www.linkedin.com/in/murrayfife

www.ingramcontent.com/pod-product-compliance
Lightning Source LLC
Chambersburg PA
CBHW080429060326

40689CB00019B/4439